Te
for

Published by:
Candlestick Press,
Diversity House, 72 Nottingham Road, Arnold, Nottingham UK NG5 6LF
www.candlestickpress.co.uk

Design and typesetting by Craig Twigg

Printed by Ratcliff & Roper Print Group, Nottinghamshire, UK

Selection © Di Slaney and Katharine Towers

Introduction © Di Slaney

Cover illustration © Alexandra Buckle, 2020
www.alexandrabuckle.co.uk

Candlestick Press monogram © Barbara Shaw, 2008

© Candlestick Press, 2020

ISBN 978 1 907598 97 5

Acknowledgements

The poems in this pamphlet are reprinted from the following books, all by permission of the publishers listed unless stated otherwise. Every effort has been made to trace the copyright holders of the poems published in this book. The editors and publisher apologise if any material has been included without permission or without the appropriate acknowledgement, and would be glad to be told of anyone who has not been consulted.

Thanks are due to all the copyright holders cited below for their kind permission:

Fiona Benson, *Bright Travellers* (Jonathan Cape, 2014). Copyright © Fiona Benson. Reproduced by permission of the author c/o Rogers, Coleridge & White Ltd., 20 Powis Mews, London W11 1JN. Louise Glück, *Faithful & Virtuous Night: Poems* (Carcanet Press, 2015). Choman Hardi, *Life for Us* (Bloodaxe Books, 2004) www.bloodaxebooks.com. Jane Kenyon, *Collected Poems* (Graywolf Press, 2005). Copyright © 2005 by The Estate of Jane Kenyon. Reprinted with the permission of The Permissions Company LLC on behalf of Graywolf Press, www.graywolfpress.org. Norman MacCaig, *The Poems of Norman MacCaig*, edited Ewen MacCaig (Polygon, 2009) by permission of PLS Clear. Aidan Carl Mathews, *Windfalls* (Dolmen Press, 1977) by kind permission of the author. Naomi Shihab Nye, *You & Yours* (BOA editions, 2005). Copyright © 2005 by Naomi Shihab Nye. Reprinted with the permission of The Permissions Company LLC on behalf of BOA Editions, Ltd., www.boaeditions.org.

All permissions cleared courtesy of Swift Permissions
swiftpermissions@gmail.com

Contents		**Page**
Introduction	*Di Slaney*	*5*
Adlestrop	*Edward Thomas*	*7*
Andraitx – Pomegranate Flowers	*DH Lawrence*	*8*
Summer roof	*Choman Hardi*	*9*
Poem for James	*Fiona Benson*	*10*
Woodniche	*Aidan Carl Mathews*	*11*
July evening	*Norman MacCaig*	*12*
Heavy Summer Rain	*Jane Kenyon*	*13*
A Summer Garden	*Louise Glück*	*14 - 18*
August 1914	*Isaac Rosenberg*	*19*
Last August Hours Before the Year 2000	*Naomi Shihab Nye*	*20*

Introduction

The extremes and contrasts of summer provide us with rich material for poetry, as we move from heat to rain, bounty to famine, rest to play, full colour to bleached white. Within this small selection of ten poems, we've tried to capture some of the beauty and passion of these longed-for months which come and go all too quickly.

We open with Thomas's famous paean to Adlestrop, perfectly capturing a gorgeous pastoral scene in June when the world held its breath at what was to come – the "burnt space through ripe fields" in Rosenberg's 'August 1914' war poem later in the selection. That sense of ripening is echoed by the setting of Lawrence's poem, where the flaming colour of pomegranate flowers seems to irradiate human desire during harvest time. Heat and desire go hand in hand – from Hardi's unconsummated yearning on a summer roof to the pulsing thunder and "unwashed skin peppery with sweat" of Benson's love poem for James.

And throughout this mini-anthology, the natural world is humming and singing, bursting with colour and renewed life – from the dragonflies in Mathews' laden suntrap woodland to the grace and simplicity of birds in MacCaig's July evening, and the unfolding beauty of Glück's magnificent garden sequence.

We hope that you will revel in the glory of these summer poems, enjoy all their tastes and smells, feel some of their heat on your skin even if summer rains beat against your window.

Di Slaney

Adlestrop

Yes, I remember Adlestrop –
The name, because one afternoon
Of heat the express-train drew up there
Unwontedly. It was late June.

The steam hissed. Someone cleared his throat.
No one left and no one came
On the bare platform. What I saw
Was Adlestrop – only the name

And willows, willow-herb, and grass,
And meadowsweet, and haycocks dry,
No whit less still and lonely fair
Than the high cloudlets in the sky.

And for that minute a blackbird sang
Close by, and round him, mistier,
Farther and farther, all the birds
Of Oxfordshire and Gloucestershire.

Edward Thomas (1878 – 1917)

Andraitx – Pomegranate Flowers

It is June, it is June,
the pomegranates are in flower,
the peasants are bending cutting the bearded wheat.

The pomegranates are in flower
beside the high road, past the deathly dust,
and even the sea is silent in the sun.

Short gasps of flame in the green of night, way off
the pomegranates are in flower,
small sharp red fires in the night of leaves.

And noon is suddenly dark, is lustrous, is silent and dark
men are unseen, beneath the shading hats;
only, from out the foliage of the secret loins
red flamelets here and there reveal
a man, a woman there.

DH Lawrence (1885 – 1930)

Summer roof

Every night that summer
when we went to bed on the flat roof,
I stayed awake
watching the opposite roof
where he was,
a tiny light turning on
every time he puffed his cigarette.

Once I was shown his paintings
and I went home
and wrote his name all over my books.

I kept imagining what he would say,
how I would respond.
I imagined being married to him,
looking after him when he fell ill,
cooking for him and washing his hair.
I imagined sleeping on the same roof.

A whole year went by and we never talked
then suddenly an empty house opposite us,
an empty roof, not staring back
and sleepless nights for me.

Years later we met again
the same man with a few fingers missing,
bad tempered, not able to paint.

We never spoke,
we remained on our separate roofs.

Choman Hardi

Poem for James

Summer; thunder pulsed on the horizon
while hummingbirds slipped through the thickened air
to circle the dropper, sip sugared water,
and I half-waded, half-swam, thigh-deep in pollen,
which rose in a haze from their meadow-grown lawn.
I was straight off the bus in that glaze of heat,
my unwashed skin peppery with sweat,
rucksack, camera, dirt, bearing me down
to the devil. But there you were, waist-deep in saffron,
your long arms folded and every hair on them
glowing like bronze, your red hair on fire
and your dark eyes attentive, though you don't remember,
which is why I'm writing it down, from the goldenrod in bloom
to your nimbus of insects lit by sun.

Fiona Benson

Woodniche

The dragonflies were here before us, friend:
Cupboard of branch and bramble, woodniche
Where the sun tumbles, foxgloves are gorgeous.
Children tore their knees among these thorns,

Fleshed their pullovers with raspberries.
Orange peel made ripples in the brown water,
Pebbles explored beyond our peering. I
Chewed dandelions and the sun brothered me.

Huge as policemen, sombre as soutanes,
The kind trees whispered in the long watch
And I used wonder in tremendous shadow
And be afraid of where the wonder led.

Summer was wealthy with a daze of suntraps,
Daffodil-spitting, sumptuous. Everywhere
Ours for the taking. Whoever has said
It is time to go home is an adult.

Aidan Carl Mathews

July evening

A bird's voice chinks and tinkles
Alone in the gaunt reedbed –
    Tiny silversmith
Working late in the evening.

    I sit and listen. The rooftop
With a quill of smoke stuck in it
    Wavers against the sky
In the dreamy heat of summer.

Flowers' closing time: bee lurches
Across the hayfield, singing
    And feeling its drunken way
Round the air's invisible corners.

And grass is grace. And charlock
Is gold of its own bounty.
    The broken chair by the wall
Is one with immortal landscapes.

Something has been completed
That everything is part of,
    Something that will go on
Being completed forever.

Norman MacCaig (1910 – 1996)

Heavy Summer Rain

The grasses in the field have toppled,
and in places it seems that a large, now
absent, animal must have passed the night.
The hay will right itself if the day

turns dry. I miss you steadily, painfully.
None of your blustering entrances
or exits, doors swinging wildly
on their hinges, or your huge unconscious
sighs when you read something sad,
like Henry Adams's letters from Japan,
where he traveled after Clover died.

Everything blooming bows down in the rain:
white irises, red peonies; and the poppies
with their black and secret centers
lie shattered on the lawn.

Jane Kenyon (1947 – 1995)

A Summer Garden

1.

Several weeks ago I discovered a photograph of my mother
sitting in the sun, her face flushed as with achievement or triumph.
The sun was shining. The dogs
were sleeping at her feet where time was also sleeping,
calm and unmoving as in all photographs.

I wiped the dust from my mother's face.
Indeed, dust covered everything; it seemed to me the persistent
haze of nostalgia that protects all relics of childhood.
In the background, an assortment of park furniture, trees, and shrubbery.

The sun moved lower in the sky, the shadows lengthened and darkened.
The more dust I removed, the more these shadows grew.
Summer arrived. The children
leaned over the rose border, their shadows
merging with the shadows of the roses.

A word came into my head, referring
to this shifting and changing, these erasures
that were now obvious –

it appeared, and as quickly vanished.
Was it blindness or darkness, peril, confusion?

Summer arrived, then autumn. The leaves turning,
the children bright spots in a mash of bronze and sienna.

2.

When I had recovered somewhat from these events,
I replaced the photograph as I had found it
between the pages of an ancient paperback,
many parts of which had been
annotated in the margins, sometimes in words but more often
in spirited questions and exclamations
meaning "I agree" or "I'm unsure, puzzled" –

The ink was faded. Here and there I couldn't tell
what thoughts occurred to the reader
but through the blotches I could sense
urgency, as though tears had fallen.

I held the book awhile.
It was *Death in Venice* (in translation);
I had noted the page in case, as Freud believed,
nothing is an accident.

Thus the little photograph
was buried again, as the past is buried in the future.
In the margin there were two words,
linked by an arrow: "sterility" and, down the page, "oblivion" –

"And it seemed to him the pale and lovely
Summoner out there smiled at him and beckoned..."

3.

How quiet the garden is;
no breeze ruffles the Cornelian cherry.
Summer has come.

How quiet it is
now that life has triumphed. The rough

pillars of the sycamores
support the immobile
shelves of the foliage,

the lawn beneath
lush, iridescent –

And in the middle of the sky,
the immodest god.

Things are, he says. They are, they do not change;
response does not change.

How hushed it is, the stage
as well as the audience; it seems
breathing is an intrusion.

He must be very close,
the grass is shadowless.

How quiet it is, how silent,
like an afternoon in Pompeii.

4.

Mother died last night,
Mother who never dies.

Winter was in the air,
many months away
but in the air nevertheless.

It was the tenth of May.
Hyacinth and apple blossom
bloomed in the back garden.

We could hear
Maria singing songs from Czechoslovakia –

How alone I am –
songs of that kind.

How alone I am,
no mother, no father –
my brain seems so empty without them.

Aromas drifted out of the earth;
the dishes were in the sink,
rinsed but not stacked.

Under the full moon
Maria was folding the washing;
the stiff sheets became
dry white rectangles of moonlight.

How alone I am, but in music
my desolation is my rejoicing.

It was the tenth of May
as it had been the ninth, the eighth.

Mother slept in her bed,
her arms outstretched, her head
balanced between them.

5.

Beatrice took the children to the park in Cedarhurst.
The sun was shining. Airplanes
passed back and forth overhead, peaceful because the war was over.

It was the world of her imagination:
true and false were of no importance.

Freshly polished and glittering –
that was the world. Dust
had not yet erupted on the surface of things.

The planes passed back and forth, bound
for Rome and Paris – you couldn't get there
unless you flew over the park. Everything
must pass through, nothing can stop –

The children held hands, leaning
to smell the roses.
They were five and seven.

Infinite, infinite – that
was her perception of time.

She sat on a bench, somewhat hidden by oak trees.
Far away, fear approached and departed;
from the train station came the sound it made.

The sky was pink and orange, older because the day was over.

There was no wind. The summer day
cast oak-shaped shadows on the green grass.

Louise Glück

August 1914

What in our lives is burnt
In the fire of this?
The heart's dear granary?
The much we shall miss?

Three lives hath one life –
Iron, honey, gold.
The gold, the honey gone –
Left is the hard and cold.

Iron are our lives
Molten right through our youth.
A burnt space through ripe fields,
A fair mouth's broken tooth.

Isaac Rosenberg (1890 – 1918)

Last August Hours Before the Year 2000

Spun silk of mercy,
long-limbed afternoon,
sun urging purple blossoms from baked stems.
What better blessing than to move without hurry
under trees?
Lugging a bucket to the rose that became a twining
house by now, roof and walls of vine –
you could live inside this rose.
Pouring a slow stream around the
ancient pineapple crowned with spiky fruit,
I thought we would feel old
by the year 2000.
Walt Disney thought cars would fly.

What a drama to keep thinking *the last summer
the last birthday*
before the calendar turns to zeroes.
My neighbor says anything we plant
in September takes hold.
She's lining pots of little grasses by her walk.

I want to know the root goes deep
on all that came before,
you could lay a soaker hose across
your whole life and know
there was something
under layers of packed summer earth
and dry blown grass
to moisten.

Naomi Shihab Nye